Strength
IN THE
Struggle

Scan this code for a
*special message from
the author,
Lauren Ibach!*

PLUS FREE BONUS!

Strength in the Struggle
© Paper Peony Press.
First Edition, 2022

Published by: Paper Peony Press
@paperpeonypress
www.paperpeonypress.com

Scripture quotations are taken from the ESV® Bible (The Holy Bible, English
Standard Version®). Copyright © 2001 by Crossway, a publishing ministry of
Good News Publishers. Used by permission. All rights reserved.

Hand-lettered artwork: Lauren Ibach

For wholesale inquiries contact: reagan@paperpeonypress.com

Printed in China

ISBN- 978-1-952842-84-9

Contents

Introduction

Hello, sweet friend. I am so grateful you picked up this book. But on the other hand, I know that you likely did because you are struggling in some way with anxiety and fear. While I don't know the specifics of your personal struggles, I know from my own experience that this is not an easy battle. But I also know that God gives us hope and equips us to face our struggles and experience freedom and victory.

My Story

Over the course of my life I have struggled with anxiety and fear in many forms. As a child, I struggled with fears that enslaved me to obsessive thoughts and compulsive behavior. My teens and early twenties were marked by depression and anxiety where I experienced intense emotions and some of the lowest lows and debilitating moments. More recently, I've become acquainted with how anxiety and fear impact me physically. I spent years in and out of therapy, on and off medications, and learning to cope in other ways. However, I really began to experience a transformation after I went through biblical counseling with my pastor and learned what it meant to be strengthened by the Spirit and how to apply God's Word to my life.

I received Christ as my Lord and Savior when I was 19 and began reading and studying the Bible pretty early on in my walk with Him. And by His grace, God began rapidly changing my heart and my life. However, during a long, challenging season when my husband was sick, I started noticing a disconnect between what I knew God said in His Word and how that applied to my life. I remember thinking during one of my lowest moments of despair: "God, I know You're sovereign, but I'm not finding any comfort in that. I don't understand what this means for me personally in this moment." Years later, God graciously led my husband and me to biblical counseling where I learned how to make those connections and it radically changed my life.

It's been a few years since that experience, but I still apply what I learned in that season today. The battle with anxiety and fear is an ongoing one in my life, but how I fight it has changed drastically and God is graciously filling me with His abundant peace, hope, and strength as I study His Word and grow in my relationship with Him.

My Hope For You

I am not an expert on anxiety and fear nor am I under the impression that I understand completely what you're experiencing just because I've been on a journey of my own. But I do hope you're comforted to know that you have a friend in this battle. I'm not here to make assumptions, insert my own opinions, or even share stories of my own experiences throughout the lessons. God is the expert on anxiety and fear and He knows every detail of your personal struggles. His Word has the power and authority to give us hope and strength in our struggles and transform our lives. Therefore, I hope to fade into the background and simply help facilitate your time in His Word—to provide context, clarity, and allow His Spirit to do a work in your heart as you answer the questions.

I trust that God will comfort and strengthen you through this study. But there will also likely be moments where He challenges you. So before diving in, I encourage you to take some time to pray. You can be open with Him about your struggles. Ask Him to comfort and strengthen you in the ways you need and that He would give you a soft, humble heart and a willingness to be challenged.

About This Study

Before diving in, I wanted to take a moment to explain the format of this study and why we will be taking this particular approach to studying the Bible. Each lesson is divided into sections to help you internalize and accurately interpret Scripture and apply it to your life.

Memory Verse

Each lesson is centered around a memory verse or short passage. You may find it tempting not to memorize, but I challenge you to take this extra step. I've heard it said that we only remember about 35% of what we study in the Bible, but we remember 100% of what we've memorized. In other words, you may not remember every last detail of what you learn in this study, but if you're memorizing the passages, you'll for sure remember the Bible verses which is no small thing!

Because all Scripture is breathed out by God and therefore is alive and active (2 Timothy 3:16, Hebrews 4:12), we can trust He will use Scripture memorization in powerful ways in our lives. When we store God's Word in our hearts, He renews our minds and uses what we've memorized to help us think and act biblically. This is especially important as we seek hope, strength, and victory in our battles against anxiety and fear. We can trust the Holy Spirit to bring to mind the verses we commit to memory when we're facing battles. In fact, the verses we're going to be studying could be considered "fighter verses" against anxiety and fear.

Each lesson opens with a verse or short passage to memorize as you study. If you need some help in this area, I've got some helpful tips for you in the following pages!

Historical Context

God speaks with intent and His Word is without error (Psalm 18:30, 2 Peter 1:20-21). Our goal is to understand His intended message to us before applying it to our lives. In order to gain an accurate understanding of what He is saying to us and how to apply it to our struggles with anxiety and fear, we first have to understand the historical context. Knowing the human author, date, setting, and audience the passage was originally written for helps us understand what God was saying in biblical times and what He is saying to us today. A passage can't mean something that it didn't mean to its original audience, so this is an important step in establishing the purpose of a passage.

In each lesson, you can expect a short commentary to give you information you may not find in your Bible, as well as a few questions to help you gain some insight through historical context revealed in Scripture.

Biblical Context

Once we've established the historical context of our memory passage, we'll move onto the biblical context. Understanding the surrounding Scripture and related verses throughout the Bible will help us learn the true meaning behind our memory verses. The commentaries and questions included in each lesson will help us gain a better understanding of the bigger picture: the purpose, main idea, and points the author was communicating. This adds accuracy to our interpretation and depth to the meaning of each memory passage.

Memory Verse

Once we've studied the historical and biblical contexts to understand the purpose and overarching message, we'll finally be ready to study our memory verses specifically. The questions and commentaries will help you reflect on the meaning within the broader context, make whole Bible connections, and consider how each passage relates to our battles with anxiety and fear.

Reflection

There are very few reflection questions leading up to this point, so here is where we'll spend a question or two simply reflecting on what we studied before moving on to the application part. This section is typically pretty short, but if you want to do more reflecting, I encourage you to journal about it in the space provided.

Application

Once we've done our due diligence in studying our memory verse within its historical and biblical contexts, we can consider how to accurately apply what we learned to our lives—specifically in our battles with anxiety and fear. God instructs us in James 1:22–25 to not only be hearers of the Word, but also doers. Growing in our knowledge of the Word is important, but God's intent is for us to live out what we learn as well. This doesn't happen automatically and applying what we learn often doesn't come easily—especially when we are struggling mentally and emotionally. However, the choice and challenge is worth it! God works in mighty ways when we apply His Word in heart, mind, and action by the power of His Spirit.

Prayer

Each lesson will close with a prayer prompt. It's the same prompt from lesson to lesson, so it may feel tempting to skip over it. But don't underestimate the power of prayer and how your prayers will change throughout the study. God hears and answers prayer, so take time to earnestly pray after each lesson and reflect on how He is working in and through you as you study and apply what you learn.

Additional Commentaries

My desire as an author is to allow the Bible to speak, because God's Word has more power than my words. However, I do provide some biblical commentary to bring clarity where needed. These commentaries are not based on my opinions, but are meant to point to greater biblical truths and help you understand how God's Word applies to your life. There are oftentimes Scripture references included within these commentaries and I encourage you to take the time to look them up in your Bible to deepen your study.

Choose a Solid Translation

Last, but certainly not least, make sure you are memorizing and reading from a solid Bible translation. Some translations interpret word-for-word, others have more of a thought-for-thought approach. It's important to get to know your Bible, so I encourage you to take the time to do an internet search and learn a bit on your own if you haven't before. I also have some helpful information on Bible translations on my blog at laurenibach.com. But for quick reference, ESV, NASB, NIV, KJV, NKJV, CSB, and NLT are just a few trusted translations. I will be referencing the ESV translation throughout the study, but feel free to study and memorize from your preferred translation.

Additionally, it's important to note that some "translations" are only paraphrases or are false altogether. Paraphrases can occasionally be a helpful addition to your personal studies, but they shouldn't be treated as your go-to Bible. And of course, we want to avoid inaccurate translations completely! Again, an internet search or visit to my blog can help you learn more.

Scripture Memory Tips

Whether you're brand new to Scripture memorization or have done it in the past, I hope these tips will be a blessing as you commit to memorizing our "fighter verses" in this study.

Why Scripture Memorization Is Important

I already talked about this at the beginning of the "About This Study" section. But to put it simply, when we memorize Scripture, we are storing God's Word in our hearts. As a result, He renews our minds and uses what we've memorized to help us think and act biblically.

Memorizing Scripture When You're Struggling Mentally and Emotionally

Since this is a study on anxiety and fear, I thought it would be helpful to talk briefly about memorizing Scripture when we're struggling mentally and emotionally. These moments can no doubt be some of the most challenging times to memorize and recall Scripture. When our thoughts are consumed with anxiety and fear, oftentimes the last thing we feel like doing is going to the Word. However, by the power of the Holy Spirit, we can learn to choose His Word even when we don't feel like it.

This is why it's important that we start with prayer. We can ask God to strengthen us by the power of His Spirit to enable us to do this. We can trust that He is faithful to answer by helping us turn to Him because this is His will for us (1 John 5:14-15)! And of course, we can rest in His abundant grace as we learn, stumble, and grow through this process.

As you go through the tips below, make realistic, doable goals. Think about the times of day or circumstances where you tend to feel better mentally and emotionally and commit to memorizing during those times. Likewise, consider where you can keep visual reminders to prompt you to recall what you've memorized in your more challenging moments. Keep in mind, God knows your struggles and weaknesses even better than you do. Ask Him to show you what you need and give you wisdom to establish a Scripture memorization battle plan!

Designate Times and Places

Memorizing Scripture requires discipline, but the verses in our study won't require a huge time commitment. It can be helpful to start by designating 5–10 minutes out of your day to begin learning a brand-new verse since this requires the most focus and oftentimes repeating it out loud. Then, once you've got it down relatively well, you can utilize other pockets of time throughout your day for review. For instance, you could dedicate a few minutes during your daily quiet time to learn a new verse, but then you could work on reviewing quietly or in your head while you're in line at the grocery store or waiting for a meeting or appointment to start. I often go on walks to learn a new passage because I feel like I have fewer mental distractions when I'm outside and moving! Try a bunch of times and places and see what works best for you. Many of us have pockets of time we don't even realize we could be using for our spiritual benefit! For instance, think about when you tend to scroll on your phone—could you replace some of that scrolling time for Scripture memorization time?

Establish Accountability

One of the biggest challenges with Scripture memorization is staying committed. This is a spiritual discipline, so it's not always going to be easy to choose to spend time on this. One of the best ways we can remain committed is to have an accountability partner. It's ideal to have someone memorize the same verses as you, but if that's not an option, simply letting a spouse, roommate, or trusted loved one know your goals can be helpful. Ask them for prayer and to ask you periodically about how it's going. Maybe even commit to sharing what you've memorized with that person if you're feeling extra confident. If you tend to struggle with self-discipline, this is a tip you definitely won't want to skip.

Notecards, Notepads, and Sticky Notes

You can simply open your Bible and start memorizing, but it can be helpful to write your verses on notecards, notepads, and/or sticky notes. The key is having your verses easily accessible. The easier they are to access, the more likely you are to learn and review. Simply write your verse reference at the top (with the translation) and then write the verse below. For longer passages, I break down each verse line by line. For particularly wordy or repetitive passages, I'll even underline or group words together.

Philippians 4:6-7 ESV

⁶ do not be anxious about anything, but in everything by prayer and supplication with thanksgiving let your requests be made known to God.

⁷ And the peace of God, which surpasses all understanding, will guard your hearts and your minds in Christ Jesus.

I personally have a designated mini notepad where I keep all my memory verses and I generally keep this on my nightstand or by my spot on the couch to reference during down times. But, I'll also write out a notecard to carry in my purse, or even put in a ziploc bag and review in the shower! (Yes, I do this sometimes!) Some people find sticky notes on their mirrors or other places they look often helpful, but I personally tend to overlook sticky notes so this doesn't work for me. As you grow in the discipline of memorizing Scripture, you'll figure out what works best for you.

Visual Tools: Drawings, Letters, and Hand Motions

If you're a visual person, you may find drawing pictures helpful as you review. You don't have to be an artist! The simplest little doodles are often all we need. If you know what the scribble means, that's all that matters. If you like using notecards, you can draw your pictures on the back to help you review and then flip the card over for the full verse to see if you got the verse right. Does drawing just not appeal to you? Instead of drawing pictures, writing the first letter of each word of the verse can be a great visual prompt for review as well! Creating hand motions to go along with your verse can also be a helpful visual reminder for some.

Audible Tools: Listening and Music

Creating a recording of yourself reading a verse and listening to it can be helpful, as can utilizing one of the many of the Bible apps and websites that have listening options. If you're the creative type, you may also find it helpful to set your verse to a rhythm or melody to aid in memorization. It doesn't have to be perfect to the ears of others, but if it helps you remember the passage, then it's perfectly serving its purpose!

Apps and Websites

There are also a variety of apps and websites to look into. You can even use a simple notes app on your phone instead of notecards. But, I personally do best with the least amount of tech involved in the Scripture memory process. I find that more tangible tools without the distractions of notifications are most helpful to me. However, I do often take pictures of my notecards and save them in a folder on my phone to reference when I don't have my actual notecard with me. Again, the goal is to find what works best for you, so if you are a super techy person, apps and websites may be your best friend.

Making Scripture Memory a Part of Your Daily Life

It's important to take time to intentionally be in God's Word and to study what we're memorizing and that's exactly what we'll be doing in this study. But I hope as you begin making Scripture memory a part of your daily life, you'll see how recalling and reflecting on the Bible throughout the day renews our minds and shapes our thoughts and actions. It's especially exciting when the Holy Spirit brings to mind verses we're memorizing in the moments we're most in need or even when someone else in our lives needs to hear a particular truth. God uses Scripture memory to bless us and those around us.

Now Let's Begin!

These tips are meant to be a blessing, not a burden. So if you're feeling overwhelmed, just pick one thing to start with and go from there. Grace abounds! Continue in prayer and trust in the Lord's faithfulness to guide you as you earnestly seek to grow in your walk with Him through Scripture memory and study. The Word of God has the power to comfort and encourage us, as well as challenge and transform us. As our hope in Christ and His Word grows, we are strengthened to face life's ongoing battles against anxiety and fear. Now let's begin.

Deliverance From Fear

Memory Verse

"I sought the LORD, and he answered me and delivered me from all my fears." — *Psalm 34:4*

Historical Context

According to the title, David is the author of this psalm. God anointed David to be king of Israel, but at the time this psalm was written, Saul was still king and he unjustly sought to kill David. 1 Samuel tells us many stories of David as he fled from Saul. And as the title of Psalm 34 indicates, David wrote it after he fled to Gath and changed his behavior before Achish (Abimilech), the king of Gath.

1. To better understand the circumstances that led David to write Psalm 34, read 1 Samuel 17:4, 24, 48–53. Then read 1 Samuel 21:10–15. Do your best to summarize what happened below.

2. According to 1 Samuel 21:12, how did David react to being recognized by Achish and his servants?

It can be tempting to skip over the historical context and just dive right into the text we want to focus on. But the title of Psalm 34 gives us a clear window into the circumstances that led David to write it. David was afraid after being recognized—he feared for his very life! Knowing this will help us as we dive into Psalm 34 and contrast what he felt with what he expressed to God.

Biblical Context

The Psalms are a collection of inspired Hebrew prayers and hymns[1] found in the middle of the Bible. There are several different types of psalms, but Psalm 34 is a psalm of thanksgiving.

3. Read Psalm 34 in its entirety and underline words that repeat. List those words below. What seems to be David's focus in this psalm? What is he praising and thanking God for?

4. Think about what David was experiencing during the time he wrote this psalm (1 Samuel 21:12). What stands out to you about what he is declaring in Psalm 34?

5. God's deliverance is a key theme in this psalm. Aside from David, who else does God deliver and from what does He deliver them? (Hint: See verses 4, 6–7, 17, and 19)

The Hebrew word for deliverance used in Psalm 34 is *nāṣal* (naw-tsal') and it means to snatch away, deliver, rescue, or save.[2] God delivered David from a dangerous situation and David gave thanks to God for rescuing him. But this points toward the greater truth that all who turn away from evil and seek God will be delivered from sin and condemnation (v. 22). This reflects Jesus's teaching in Mark 1:15 that in order to be saved, we must repent and believe in him. When we truly believe in Jesus, we will turn from our sinful thoughts and actions, and align our hearts to His and what He says in His Word. He will deliver us from our greatest fears: death and condemnation.

Psalm 34 tells us that God delivers the righteous from all fears, troubles, and afflictions. How can that be, when bad things still happen in our lives? Let's look at this promise in light of the gospel. When we put our faith in Christ, He instantly takes away the guilt of our sin and declares us righteous in His sight. We are immediately rescued from the penalty of our sin and given eternal life (Romans 6:23). When Jesus returns to dwell with His people, there will be no more sorrow or pain (Revelation 21:4). If God has the power to do this, then He has the power to deliver us from all other fears!

When our eyes are fixed on Christ and the gospel, He delivers us from all fears, because we know that our future is secure in Him.

Memory Verse

As David fled for his life, he may have been afraid, but he kept his focus on God. David praised God for who He is and what He promised, and gave thanks to the Lord for answering his prayers. Keeping in mind the historical and biblical contexts of Psalm 34, let's now dive a bit deeper into our memory verse.

6. Read Psalm 34:4 and paraphrase it in your own words.

7. What difference do you notice between the fear mentioned in verse 4 and the fear mentioned in verses 7, 9, and 11?

Fear vs. Fearing the Lord

The Hebrew word used in Psalm 34:4 that refers to the fears God delivered David from is *mᵉḡôrâ* (meg-o-raw') and it means fear or terror.[3] In contrast, there's a different word used in verse 7 that refers to the fear of the Lord. That word is *yārē'* (yaw-ray') and it describes reverent fear.[4] In Psalm 34:4, David is thanking God for delivering him from a terrifying circumstance. He goes on to praise the Lord and call others to revere Him. Simply put, God delivers us from our fears when we reverently fear Him.

Reflection

Let's take a moment to reflect on what we just studied.

8. What did you learn from studying Psalm 34? How do these truths speak into your own battles against fear and anxiety?

Application

Now that we better understand the context and meaning of our memory verse, let's apply what we've learned to our own lives.

9. In what ways are you in need of deliverance from fear? What fears are you most struggling with in this season of your life? Write them below.

10. How do you currently respond to those fears? In what ways are they impacting your life?

11. Fear of the Lord makes deliverance from fear possible. How does knowing that God is our Deliverer change the way you think about your fear? Is there a step you need to take by faith?

Prayer

Take a moment to pray about what you studied. Praise God for who He is, thank Him for what He taught you in this lesson, confess any sins that came to mind, and trust you are forgiven in Christ. Then ask Him to help you apply what you learned to your life in thought and action. Feel free to write that prayer below.

I sought the Lord, and he answered me and delivered me from all my fears. Psalm 34:4

 **Lesson 2**

> ### Memory Verse
>
> *"If then you have been raised with Christ, seek the things that are above, where Christ is, seated at the right hand of God. Set your minds on things that are above, not on things that are on earth. For you have died, and your life is hidden with Christ in God. When Christ who is your life appears, then you also will appear with him in glory." — Colossians 3:1–4*

Historical Context

Colossians is a letter written by the Apostle Paul to the church in Colossae, a small city at the base of Mt. Cadmus in Asia Minor, and now known as the city of Honaz in modern-day Turkey.[5] The letter was written around 62 AD while Paul was imprisoned in Rome, approximately 30 years after Christ's death and resurrection. Scholars can only speculate the specific reasons that this letter was written, but we do know that false teaching among the church at Colossae minimized Jesus's power, authority, and the new identity believers have in Him. Paul wrote this letter as a warning, but also as an encouragement to the believers to live in union with Christ and grow in spiritual maturity.[6]

1. The truths about Christ's power and authority were being diminished, but Paul corrected this early on in his letter. Read Colossians 1:15–16 and list the words and phrases Paul used to describe Jesus.

2. Read Colossians 2:8. What is Paul's warning to the church? In what ways were they being deceived and why?

When we forget who God is, our faith becomes shaky and we're more vulnerable to accept and develop inaccurate ideas about Him. We see this exemplified in the Colossian church, which is why Paul promptly addresses and corrects the false teachings about Christ. Knowing and regularly reflecting on the attributes of God is foundational to having a strong faith. Doing so glorifies God and protects us from having a distorted view of Him. Not only that, but when our trust in His character increases, our fears, anxieties, and discontentments decrease. We are transformed as we learn to view all things in light of who He is!

Biblical Context

The Apostle Paul's letter to the Colossians is also called an epistle, a letter written to a church or individual for a specific occasion. Paul authored thirteen of the twenty-one epistles in the New Testament. Epistles follow a general form: a greeting, prayer and thanksgiving, a body, and closing greeting. We will be studying a section of the body of this epistle, where Paul addresses some of the teachings that were circulating and how believers should respond.

Read Colossians 2:20–3:17.

3. In Colossians 2:20–23, we catch a glimpse of some of the false teachings and regulations that were deceiving the church. How does Paul describe these teachings?

4. How does Paul exhort the believers to respond in Colossians 3:1–14? What must they "put to death" and what must they "put on" and why?

5. How does "being renewed" (v. 10) both encourage and comfort you in your battles with anxiety and fear?

6. According to chapter 3, verses 15–16, what needs to rule and dwell in the hearts of believers in order to do all to God's glory (v. 17)?

Memory Verse

Paul gets to the heart of the matter in our memory passage. Read Colossians 3:1–4.

7. What is true for those who are in Christ and how should believers respond to that reality?

8. What does it mean to be hidden with Christ in God (v. 3)? (Read also Romans 6:1–11, Galatians 2:20 and 2 Corinthians 5:17.)

As the Colossian believers were persuaded by false teachings, they lost sight of their identity in Christ. Though alive in Him, they were acting as if they were still dead in their sin. When Paul admonished them to put to death the old self and put on the new self, he wasn't saying, "follow these rules and you will be saved." Remember, he was speaking to believers who were already saved. He was encouraging them to live in the fullness of their identity in Christ!

Like the Colossians, we too can develop wrong beliefs about God and lose sight of who we are in Christ. The Bible teaches that we are all sinners (Romans 3:23) and that "the wages of sin is death" (Romans 6:23). Jesus paid the penalty for our sins when He died on the cross, and He rose from the dead for our justification (Romans 4:25). In other words, His righteousness is credited to our account—we are declared righteous in His sight and given new life! This is our identity as believers. So even though we still struggle with sin on this side of eternity, those who receive Christ as Lord and Savior never have to question their standing with God or His power and authority over our weaknesses and sin. We are hidden with Christ in God!

Reflection

Let's take a moment to reflect on what we just studied.

9. How do false beliefs about God impact anxiety and fear?

10. What strategies does the world tell you to implement in your life in order to deal with anxiety and fear? How does it differ from what God offers?

Application

Now that we better understand the context and meaning of our memory verse, let's apply what we've learned to our own lives.

11. How can you apply Paul's warnings and encouragements to the Colossians in your own life?

12. What truths about God do you struggle to believe? How might reflecting on His attributes and promises strengthen you in your battles against anxiety and fear?

13. How does the knowledge that your life is hidden with Christ in God help you in the battle against anxiety and fear?

Prayer

Take a moment to pray about what you studied. Praise God for who He is, thank Him for what He taught you in this lesson, confess any sins that came to mind, and trust you are forgiven in Christ. Then ask Him to help you apply what you learned to your life in thought and action. Feel free to write that prayer below.

Hidden with Christ in God

COLOSSIANS 3:3

Lesson 3

Memory Verse

"But he said to me, 'My grace is sufficient for you, for my power is made perfect in weakness.' Therefore I will boast all the more gladly of my weaknesses, so that the power of Christ may rest upon me."
— 2 Corinthians 12:9

Historical Context

In addition to Colossians, Paul also wrote 2 Corinthians. He wrote this letter while in Macedonia around 55–56 AD, about a year or so after writing 1 Corinthians.[7] According to Acts 18:11, Paul spent a year and a half in Corinth ministering to the Jews and Gentiles (non-Jews) and establishing a church. However, after Paul left to continue his missionary journey, problems arose among the Corinthian believers (1 Corinthians 1:11). False teachers deceived them and caused them to question Paul's authority as an apostle. He addressed these issues in letters and during a "painful visit" (2 Corinthians 2:1). As a result, most of the Corinthians realized their errors and wanted reconciliation with Paul.[8] Paul's purpose in writing 2 Corinthians was to encourage the believers who had repented and to urge the minority who still rejected Paul and his teachings to repent before he returned for another visit.[9]

1. Read Acts 18:1–17 and list the main events that happened while Paul was living in Corinth. What stands out to you about his time there?

2. In Acts 18:9–10, God spoke to Paul in a vision. What did God command Paul and what were God's promises to him?

Corinth was a wealthy, bustling urban city located in southern Greece, about 45 miles west of Athens.[10] As a Roman colony on a major trade route, Corinth was home to people who held all sorts of cultural and religious beliefs. Many speakers and social commentators would come to captivate citizens and discuss how to progress as a society.[11] The Corinthian believers faced many cultural temptations—including idolatry, sexual immorality, and pride. Not only that, false teachers had infiltrated the church and led many astray.

Even though we are far removed from Corinth by both time and geography, we can still make significant cultural comparisons and understand how the Corinthian church was influenced by the cultural beliefs of their day. One might argue that we have even more cultural temptations today because of the internet. All kinds of opinions and beliefs are constantly being exchanged through social media and digital entertainment. And as Paul warned the Corinthian believers, we too need to watch out for teachers and influencers who claim to be Christians, but don't truly believe in Christ or follow the teachings of the Bible. Like the Corinthians, we need to continually study the Word of God and pray for God to give us wisdom and discernment.

Biblical Context

2 Corinthians comes after 1 Corinthians in the New Testament. Paul communicated with the believers in Corinth on other occasions and a lot happened in the year between the writing of each letter.

2 Corinthians can be split into three parts. First, Paul defended his authority and legitimacy as an apostle (1:1–7:16). Secondly, he addressed those in the church who had repented (8:1–9:15). Finally, he addressed those who were still rejecting him and the gospel (10:1–13:10).[12] We will study chapters 11 and 12, where Paul highlighted his concerns about a group he sarcastically called "super-apostles," false teachers who claimed to have greater authority than Paul and who were wooing the Corinthians with their stories of supernatural experiences.

Read 2 Corinthians 11 and 12:1–10.

3. Throughout these chapters, Paul gave examples that proved his authority as an apostle and the validity of his message (the gospel). Why was he doing this? To whom was he comparing the false apostles to? (2 Corinthians 11:3, 12–15)

Since the false teachers boasted about supernatural experiences, Paul opened chapter 12 with his own story. However, his motives in telling that story were not the same as the "super-apostles." He wanted to make a distinction between what the false teachers valued and what he valued.

4. What did Paul boast about and what does that highlight about what the world values versus what God values?

5. Paul metaphorically spoke of a "thorn in his flesh." (v. 7) The Bible doesn't tell us exactly what that was, but how did God use that in Paul's life for good? Even though he pleaded with God to take the thorn away, what was Paul's final response? (v. 10)

Common Thorns

Real-time access to current events, the busyness of our culture, and stress of everyday life can all cause anxiety and fear. A quick internet search reveals handfuls of studies reporting on the rise of anxiety and depression among believers and unbelievers alike. While we can avoid some stress-inducing circumstances, when it comes down to it, we can't escape them all. We live in a fallen world. We might even view fear and anxiety as a thorn in our flesh—a struggle or battle we can never seem to overcome. But, there is hope for those who are in Christ! Let's continue in our study to receive encouragement directly from God's Word and learn how we can respond to these "thorns" biblically.

Memory Verse

Paul gets to the heart of the matter in our memory passage. Read 2 Corinthians 12:9.

6. How does God describe his grace and power?

7. Why does Paul say he will boast in his weaknesses? How do our weaknesses bring glory to God?

Strengthened By Christ

Without Christ, we are all dead in sin, but He died on a cross and rose from the dead so that all who turn from their sins and trust in Him will be forgiven. By His grace we are saved through faith, not by our own strength or efforts (Ephesians 2:8–9). The gospel is ultimately the story of our weakness, the sufficiency of God's grace, and His power over sin and Satan. In this truth, we have great hope for the future, and good news for the present.

Our souls long for heaven and the Bible promises that one day there will be no more sin, crying, mourning, or pain for those who are in Christ (Revelation 21:4). As we wait eagerly for that day, we can experience victory in our daily battles—including our struggles with anxiety and fear. We may already feel defeated or defined by these weaknesses. But we can be strengthened in Christ by clinging to what's true: Jesus is victorious and our identity is in Him alone.

There is no condemnation for those who are in Christ (Romans 8:1). So, we can confess our weaknesses, worries, and fears to God, ask Him to deepen our trust in Him through His Word, and be strengthened by Jesus's abundant grace (2 Timothy 2:1).

Reflection

Let's take a moment to reflect on what we just studied.

8. How does what the Bible says about weakness differ from what the world says about it? List examples that come to mind.

Application
Now that we better understand the context and meaning of our memory verse, let's apply what we've learned to our own lives.

9. How do inaccurate beliefs about God's grace impact our response to anxiety and fear? How does that change when we hold fast to biblical beliefs about God's grace, power, and strength?

10. Is anxiety and/or fear a "thorn in your flesh?" How does this passage equip and encourage you today as you face ongoing battles?

11. How might God be leading you to respond differently to circumstances that trigger anxiety and fear?

Prayer
Take a moment to pray about what you studied. Praise God for who He is, thank Him for what He taught you in this lesson, confess any sins that came to mind, and trust you are forgiven in Christ. Then ask Him to help you apply what you learned to your life in thought and action.

My grace is sufficient for you, for my power is made perfect in weakness

2 Corinthians 12:9

 **Lesson 4** **The Spirit of Fear vs. The Spirit of God**

Historical Context

2 Timothy is a letter written by the Apostle Paul to his disciple Timothy. Scholars debate on when it was written, but it was sometime between 64–67 AD. During this time, Paul was imprisoned in Rome for proclaiming the gospel, and his circumstances looked bleak. Many of His friends had abandoned him out of fear of being persecuted and he knew his execution was drawing near. So, Paul asked Timothy to come visit him one last time (2 Timothy 4:9). Paul's primary purpose for writing this letter was to encourage Timothy to remain faithful to the gospel and sound teaching and to courageously minister to others despite threats of persecution.

1. Throughout this letter, we get a clear picture of Paul's circumstances.

a. Read 2 Timothy 2:9, 4:13, and 4:16. What were the conditions in Paul's cell? How must he have felt physically?

b. How does that compare to his mindset spiritually? (Read 2 Timothy 4:17–18)

2. Read 2 Timothy 2:8–9 again. Who and what did Paul encourage Timothy to remember?

Before Jesus ascended to heaven after his resurrection, he gave his disciples the "Great Commission": to go into the world, proclaim the gospel, and make disciples of all nations (Mark 16:15, Matthew 28:19). Paul encouraged Timothy to be bold in doing this without fear of persecution. But Paul also told him in 2 Timothy 2:8–9 to "remember" the gospel—the message that Jesus died and rose from the dead to save all who repent and believe in Him (Mark 1:15). Paul knew Timothy hadn't forgotten, so why did Paul tell him to do this?

The gospel has great power in the lives of believers and Paul knew this from experience. Even though practically everything had been stripped from him, the gospel remained the source of his hope. He suffered, but he was not defeated. He trusted in the person and promises of Jesus and could see the impacts of God's grace and mercy each day. This strengthened him.

We too can forget the power of the gospel in our daily lives. We tend to have a better grasp on how it impacts us when we're saved and in the future when Jesus returns, but it can be challenging to see the impact the gospel has on the time between those two events. To paraphrase what one author said, the only way we can overwhelm the things that overwhelm us—fear and anxiety, self-condemnation, the lies of the world and Satan—is by preaching the gospel to ourselves daily.[13]

Biblical Context

2 Timothy comes after 1 Timothy in the New Testament. Most Bible interpreters agree 2 Timothy was the Apostle Paul's final epistle.[14] While Paul's letters to Titus and Philemon come after 2 Timothy in the Bible, they were written before this letter.

2 Timothy is a short epistle with just four chapters, but it's packed with truths that encourage us today. We can divide this letter into three sections. Paul opens and closes his letter with encouragement to Timothy. But in the middle section, he also warns against false teachers. We will mainly be focusing on the first part of the letter where Paul exhorts Timothy to continue courageously proclaiming the gospel.

Read 2 Timothy 1:1–14.

3. Paul exhorts Timothy not to be ashamed of what? Why is Paul unashamed? (Hint: See verses 8 and 12.) Note the way Paul talks about his belief in verse 12. How would you describe Paul's faith?

4. In verses 13-14, what does Paul tell Timothy to follow? Why is this important? (See also 2 Timothy 3:16)

5. Who indwells us and guards the Word of God within us?

Memory Verse

Paul gets to the heart of the matter in our memory passage. Read 2 Timothy 1:7.

6. What spirit comes from God and what spirit does not?

Read Galatians 5:22–23.

7. a. What similarities do you notice between this passage and our memory verse?

b. Where do these characteristics come from? Can we produce them ourselves?

Our God is one God, three Persons—Father, Son, and Holy Spirit—equal in power, holiness, and eternal nature. The Holy Spirit permanently indwells our hearts when we receive Christ as Lord and Savior (Ephesians 1:13–14, Romans 8:11). By His power alone we're able to think and live according to His will and bear good fruit (Romans 8:5–8, Galatians 2:20).

We can never lose the Holy Spirit once we're saved. However, learning to live Spirit-filled lives is an ongoing, daily process. To be filled with the Spirit is simply to be empowered and directed by Him and doesn't happen automatically. In order to be filled with the Spirit, we must be willing to live fully surrendered to Jesus, desire to honor Him with our lives, and confess our sins directly to Him, trusting He is faithful to forgive us (1 John 1:9). When we humble ourselves before the Lord, we can simply ask to be filled with the Spirit and trust He has filled us. Why? Because God commands us to be filled with the Spirit (Ephesians 5:18) and when we pray according to God's will, we know that we have what we've asked of Him (1 John 5:14–15).[15]

We are strengthened in Christ when we're rooted in the Word of God and filled with the Spirit. Battling fear and anxiety in our own strength leads to weariness and defeat. But when we're directed and empowered by the Spirit, our lives are transformed. His perfect love replaces fear with self-control to guard our thoughts and strength to overcome our daily battles (1 John 4:18, 2 Timothy 1:7).

Reflection

Let's take a moment to reflect on what we just studied.

8. Keeping in mind his circumstances, how do Paul's teachings in this letter inspire you?

Application

Now that we better understand the context and meaning of our memory verse, let's apply what we've learned to our own lives.

9. What does Paul's emphasis on God's Word and the Holy Spirit tell you about the importance of their role in your battles against fear? What difference does that make in your life?

10. Are you currently in the habit of preaching the gospel to yourself daily? If not, what might that look like for you? What are some ways you can begin reflecting more regularly?

11. Are you living a Spirit-filled life? Is there a desire you need God to change in your heart or something you need to surrender or confess to Him? Take a moment to bring those things to God in prayer.

12. Are there changes you need to make in your life to allow God to deepen your trust in Him and better equip you against anxiety and fear?

Prayer

Take a moment to pray about what you studied. Praise God for who He is, thank Him for what He taught you in this lesson, confess any sins that came to mind, and trust you are forgiven in Christ. Then ask Him to help you apply what you learned to your life in thought and action. Feel free to write that prayer below.

God gave us a spirit not of fear but of power and love and self-control.

2 Timothy 1:7

Lesson 5

"Trust in the LORD with all your heart, and do not lean on your own understanding. In all your ways acknowledge him, and he will make straight your paths." — Proverbs 3:5–6

Historical Context

Much of the book of Proverbs was written by King Solomon, who ruled Israel from 971–931 BC. Chapters 1–9 and 25–29 were his writings, but he likely simply gathered the rest of the wise sayings throughout the book.[16] Many scholars believe the book of Proverbs was not completed in full as we know it today until the days of King Hezekiah (715–686 BC) or after. In short, this unique book contains brief sayings that inform and instruct us how to live wise, godly lives.

1. Read 1 Kings 3:5–14. When Solomon became king of Israel, what did God say to Solomon and what was Solomon's request? How did God respond?

2. Read 1 Kings 4:29–34. How does the Bible describe Solomon's wisdom?

What is Wisdom?

Many in the world look at wisdom as acquired knowledge through life experiences or intentional study. But the Bible makes a distinction between worldly wisdom and godly wisdom. The Hebrew word for wisdom, *ḥāḵmâ* (khok-maw'),[17] is much more than mere intelligence or the lessons we learn throughout our lives. The word refers to skill, or applied knowledge.[18]

It pleased God when Solomon asked for wisdom. Likewise, it pleases God when we ask Him for wisdom. James 1:5 says, "If any of you lacks wisdom, let him ask God, who gives generously to all without reproach, and it will be given him." In order to receive godly wisdom, we must ask God for it through prayer, seek knowledge in His Word, and by the power of the Spirit, faithfully apply what we learn to our lives.

Biblical Context

The book of Proverbs can be found in the middle of the Bible just after the Psalms. It's a collection of wise sayings to live by, but due to their pithy and poetic nature, proverbs can easily be misinterpreted. As we read the surrounding context of our memory verse, it's important to remember that proverbs are not necessarily promises. My pastor, Troy Dobbs, clarified this so well when he explained that promises are God's guarantees to us, while proverbs are universal observations about things that are generally true. This in itself can be very confusing, but we'll keep it simple for this brief portion of our study. So as you read this section of Scripture, focus on the fact that God is communicating to us that these are wise principles for us to live by.

There are different sections of the book of Proverbs, but we will be focusing on chapter three, which falls in the first major section of the book. It's written from the perspective of a father who is speaking to his son about what it means to be wise.

Read Proverbs 3:1–12.

3. What does the father character tell his son to do in verse 1? What does this communicate to readers about what he's about to say?

4. What is the purpose of the heart in the context of this passage? (See verses 1, 3, and 5.)

The Heart

When we read the Bible, it's important to pay attention to words that repeat. The father character in this proverb repeats the word "heart" three times in these twelve verses. In doing so, he is emphasizing that trusting the Lord and obeying His commands are matters of the heart.

The Hebrew word for heart in this passage is *lēb* (labe) and it refers to the inner self—the mind, will, heart, soul, understanding, and conscience as a whole.[19] God is teaching us through this proverb that trusting Him means more than casual allegiance to Him. There is a distinction between merely knowing about God and truly knowing Him personally. This is true throughout the Bible and it's the essence of following Jesus. He said in John 14:23 that those who love Him will obey His Word. He was not implying that our works contribute to our salvation. Rather, He was emphasizing that if we truly know Him, we will love Him with our whole selves—in thought and action.

Memory Verse

We get to the main point of this passage in our memory verses. Read Proverbs 3:5–6.

5. a. What does this passage say we should do? List some examples of what it looks like to do this biblically. (Hint: Look back on what you've learned about in previous lessons.)

   b. What does this passage say we shouldn't do? List some examples of what that might look like in your own life.

6. What does it look like to fully acknowledge or submit our understanding to God? (Read Psalm 18:30, Psalm 145:17b–19, Acts 3:19, 2 Corinthians 10:3–5, and James 4:6–8.)

Trusting God

Proverbs 3:5–6 is relatively straightforward in comparison to some of the other proverbs. However, there is still plenty to unpack in our memory passage. God commands us to trust Him completely. To trust the Lord in this way is to have confidence in Him and feel safe and secure in Him.[20] We cannot do this while simultaneously trusting in our own thoughts, emotions, opinions, and ideas. We have a choice to make. But God teaches us through this proverb that if we acknowledge Him—meaning we know and submit to Him—then He will straighten our paths. This is not a promise that God will make the road in life a smooth and easy one if we have enough faith. Instead, it means that when we surrender to God, He will faithfully guide us to live according to His moral will.

God knows that we cannot perfectly trust Him with all our hearts. We make mistakes, we forget who He is and what He promises, and we sin against Him even when we don't mean to. But in Christ we are redeemed! When we trust Him as Lord and Savior, turn from our sin and our own understanding, and live according to His will and way, He will make our crooked paths straight. In Him, our destination is secure.

Reflection

Let's take a moment to reflect on what we just studied.

7. What attributes of God can you pull from Proverbs 3:5–6? How does who He is inform your understanding of your personal fears and anxieties?

Application

Now that we better understand the context and meaning of our memory verse, let's apply what we've learned to our own lives.

8. How do the principles in our memory verse differ from cultural messages about wisdom? Do those messages align with what the Bible says about wisdom? How can you navigate this in your daily life?

9. In what ways are you currently putting your trust in God into action? In what ways are you struggling to do that? What are some steps you can start taking today to grow?

10. When you're feeling anxious or fearful, where do you run for wisdom, guidance, and comfort? How can you remain or get into the habit of turning to God first?

11. What biblical truths will you choose to trust when your thoughts, emotions, or circumstances are leading you down a path towards anxiety and fear?

Prayer

Take a moment to pray about what you studied. Praise God for who He is, thank Him for what He taught you in this lesson, confess any sins that came to mind, and trust you are forgiven in Christ. Then ask Him to help you apply what you learned to your life in thought and action.

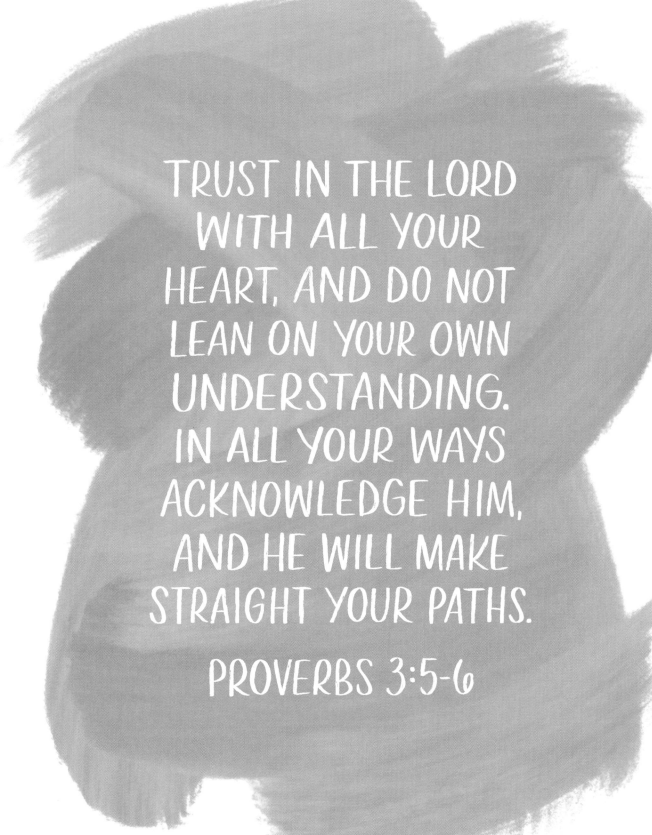

TRUST IN THE LORD WITH ALL YOUR HEART, AND DO NOT LEAN ON YOUR OWN UNDERSTANDING. IN ALL YOUR WAYS ACKNOWLEDGE HIM, AND HE WILL MAKE STRAIGHT YOUR PATHS.

PROVERBS 3:5-6

"Look at the birds of the air: they neither sow nor reap nor gather into barns, and yet your heavenly Father feeds them. Are you not of more value than they?" — *Matthew 6:26*

Historical Context

There isn't an author included in the original manuscript, but historical documents and early church tradition attribute the Gospel of Matthew to Matthew the tax collector, one of Jesus's twelve apostles. In other words, Matthew was there for many of the stories he recounted. We don't know the exact date of writing, but it was likely compiled between 55–65 AD, twenty to thirty years after Jesus's death and resurrection. Each Gospel account was written to a specific audience and highlights different themes and aspects of who Jesus is. Matthew was primarily writing to the Jews, highlighting the prophecies that prove Jesus is the long-awaited Messiah—the promised King and Savior of the world.

Matthew opens with a genealogy. At face value, this may seem like a boring or overwhelming way to begin, but it's actually quite exciting how it sets the stage for what we're about to read.

1. In 2 Samuel 7, God makes a covenant with David. Read 2 Samuel 7:12, 16–17, and Matthew 1:1–17, 28:18. What does the covenant and genealogy reveal about Jesus and His authority?

Biblical Context

Matthew is the first book of the New Testament and one of four Gospels. The word "gospel" comes from the Greek word euangelion (yoo-ang-ghel'-ee-on) which means "good news." Simply put, the Gospels tell the good news about Jesus's life, death, and resurrection—the most significant events of all time.[21] While the Gospel of Matthew tells a story, it doesn't read like a typical narrative. It's a compilation of Jesus's teachings and significant events that are brilliantly organized to show us that Jesus truly is the Messiah and King of Kings.

Matthew can be divided into several sections, but we will be focusing on a portion of Jesus's famous Sermon on the Mount. This sermon was and remains a call to faith and salvation. Jesus is illustrating that no one can measure up to God's perfect moral standard. Therefore, we need a Savior who will extend divine grace.[22] The portion of this sermon we will be focusing on is in chapter 6, where Jesus addresses worry and anxiety.

Read Matthew 6:25–34.

2. a. Jesus gives us examples that illustrate why we don't need to worry. What are they?

    b. What do these reasons reveal about His character? List the attributes of God you see exemplified in this passage.

3. What does anxiety reveal about us? How does Jesus describe us when we worry? (v. 30)

4. Read the second "Biblical Context" paragraph again. What is Jesus ultimately trying to get us to see about ourselves and about Him by pointing out our weakness?

5. In verse 33, how does Jesus inform us to respond to anxiousness? Write it in your own words.

No Condemnation for Those Who Are in Christ

When Jesus said, "O you of little faith," He was not talking about a total absence of faith. The original Greek word used here is *oligopistos* (ol-ig-op'-is-tos), which literally means "trusting too little."[23] Jesus was making it clear that when we struggle with worry and anxiety—which we all do to some extent—it reveals a lack of trust in Him. There is a difference between someone who lacks faith in Christ entirely and someone who has saving faith, but struggles to trust. There is no condemnation for those who are in Christ and wrestle with anxiety (Romans 8:1).

Jesus's purpose in pointing out our lack of trust was not to condemn, but to help us see our need for His all-sufficient grace (John 3:17). He knows that pointing out our weaknesses stings, but He does so to lovingly discipline us (1 Corinthians 11:32, Hebrews 12:5–11) and the purpose of godly discipline is to set us back on the right path. Anxiety is not God's will for us. So while we are covered in His perfect grace through faith, He is also calling us to trust Him. He is calling us to live differently than the world does (Matthew 6:31–33)—to trust Him with the forgiveness of our sins all the way down to the intricate details of our everyday lives and our most basic needs.

Memory Verse

Let's take a moment to dive a little deeper into our memory verse. Read Matthew 6:26.

6. Why are we more valuable than the rest of God's creation? (Read Genesis 1:26–31.)

7. Do you trust that God loves you and cares for you? How should an accurate understanding of our value before God impact our anxieties?

Our Sovereign Provider

From the very beginning, God has been sovereign over the lives of individuals. We read about how He made us in His image and gave humankind dominion over the animals and gave us plants for food (Genesis 1:26–31). In Eden, Adam and Eve had everything they needed. Most importantly, they had perfect fellowship with God. But when they sinned against Him, the earth was cursed and that fellowship was broken. Yet God remained faithful to His image-bearers. By His grace, He continued to provide for their earthly needs. But even more significantly, He sovereignly put a plan into motion to provide for our greatest need—salvation from sin and death—so that we could be reunited with Him. Throughout the years, people sinned and disasters happened, but He providentially orchestrated all of it to fulfill His plan.

Fast forward to our passage. Here is Jesus—the fulfillment of God's sovereign plan—standing on a mountainside, preaching to a crowd, and to us. Who better to teach us about trusting in His provision than the One who came to meet our greatest need? To be clear, His teaching doesn't mean Christians won't suffer or lack basic needs. What God wants us to know is that there is more to life than temporal things and that He is faithful to care for His children even through suffering. And just like He worked all things together to fulfill His promise and plan to save sinners, He can and will work all things together for good in the lives of those who love Him (Romans 8:28). He is our Sovereign Provider.

Reflection

Let's take a moment to reflect on what we just studied.

8. Finish these sentences:

God is my Sovereign Provider, therefore...

Jesus died on the cross for me, therefore...

God made me in His image, therefore....

Application

Now that we better understand the context and meaning of our memory verse, let's apply what we've learned to our own lives.

9. a. What do you worry most about? What makes you anxious? When you worry, where is your focus?

b. What does that reveal about your priorities? Are you trusting in something or someone more than Christ? Do you treasure something or someone more than Him?

c. How will you redirect your focus to Christ when faced with worry and anxiety?

10. Go back to question 2b and re-read the attributes you wrote down. Add any more that came to mind as you studied. If God is truly all of these things, then how will you respond?

11. How has studying this passage in the context of Jesus's call to salvation and our need for His grace encouraged you? Will you trust in the sufficiency of His grace today?

Prayer

Take a moment to pray about what you studied. Praise God for who He is, thank Him for what He taught you in this lesson, confess any sins that came to mind, and trust you are forgiven in Christ. Then ask Him to help you apply what you learned to your life in thought and action.

LOOK AT THE
BIRDS OF THE AIR...
ARE YOU NOT OF
MORE VALUE THAN THEY?

MATTHEW 6:26

Casting Our Anxieties On Him

┌─────────── **Memory Verse** ───────────┐

"Humble yourselves, therefore, under the mighty hand of God so that at the proper time he may exalt you, casting all your anxieties on him, because he cares for you." — 1 Peter 5:6–7

└───┘

Historical Context

1 Peter is a letter written by the Apostle Peter, likely while he was in Rome sometime between 62–65 AD. Unlike the other epistles we've studied, this letter wasn't written to just one church or person. It was sent to several churches in Asia Minor (modern-day Turkey). Peter's purpose in writing to all of these Gentile (non-Jewish) believers was to encourage them in the faith as they faced heavy persecution from the Greeks and Romans.

1. Acts 4:1–22 gives us a glimpse at how Peter handled persecution. What do you learn about him? What made him the way he was?

Biblical Context

1 Peter is found towards the end of the New Testament, after the book of James and before 2 Peter. It has five chapters, but can also be broken down into three core sections. First, Peter addresses what it means to be Gentile believers. Secondly, he explains what it looks like to live as Christians in a world that is hostile to them. And thirdly, he specifically encourages the believers to persevere in their suffering. We will be focusing on that final section.

Read 1 Peter 4:12–5:11.

2. Write down the words Peter uses to describe how believers should respond to persecution in 1 Peter 4:12–19. What do you find significant about these words?

3. a. According to 1 Peter 5:6–11, what action steps should believers take to resist the devil? See also Ephesians 6:10–18.

   b. According to Peter and Paul, how should believers view their trials? (Hint: See Ephesians 6:12.)

A Spiritual Battle

Many of us treat anxiety merely as a circumstantial issue. We try to avoid situations that trigger us and we look to the world for solutions to treat and manage our symptoms. But while many of these things can help us, they typically don't lead us to the root of our anxieties. The world can help us manage and cope, but what Jesus offers us is far greater.

Jesus gives us armor to protect us and divinely powerful weapons to destroy the stronghold of anxiety in our lives. When we clothe ourselves with truth, righteousness, the gospel, faith, and salvation, we are protected. And by the power of the Spirit, God's Word and prayer are our greatest weapons to take every anxious thought captive to obey Christ (Ephesians 6:10–18, 2 Corinthians 10:3–5).

Anxiety is first and foremost a spiritual battle. Before turning to the world for our answers, the believer should first turn to God. This is why we're memorizing and studying Scripture. It's why we're reflecting on the gospel and praying about what we're learning in this study. His armor and weapons have divine power not only to equip us for battle, but to change us from the inside out. We are warned against conforming to the way the world views anxiety because God has greater plans in store for us. When we do battle His way, He will transform us by renewing our minds (Romans 12:2).

Memory Verse

Let's take a moment to dive a little deeper into our memory verse.

4. "The mighty hand of God" is a phrase symbolizing God's sovereign purpose.[24] How does that explanation change your understanding of this verse?

5. Look up and write down the dictionary definition for the word "exalt." How is a believer exalted? Who ultimately gets exalted? (Read Psalm 75:6–7, Luke 14:7–11, and 1 Peter 5:10–11.)

6. What must believers do before they cast their anxieties on the Lord?

7. Why can we give all our worries, fears, and cares to God?

Casting Our Anxieties On Him

God is calling believers to submit themselves to His sovereign plan for their lives and to surrender their anxieties to Him. This doesn't come naturally to us—especially when we don't understand what God is doing in our lives and in the world around us. Oftentimes, we lay our cares and concerns at the feet of Jesus only to pick them back up again. This passage reveals why we do that and ultimately it comes down to our own pride. We are unable to truly cast our anxieties on Him when we're still holding onto our own understanding, thinking we know better, and desiring to be in control of our lives. Therefore, we must humble ourselves before God.

The verb "humble" in this passage is the Greek word *tapeinoō* (tap-i-no'-o) and it means to make low, assign a lower rank or place, and bring down one's pride.[25] To put it simply, humbling ourselves is acknowledging that Jesus is God and we are not—it's allowing Him to rule and reign in every area of our lives. He alone is all-wise, all-knowing, and fully in control. He cares for us. Therefore, we can humbly and confidently lay our anxieties before Him and trust that He will graciously restore, confirm, strengthen, and establish us even through suffering and uncertainty (1 Peter 5:10).

Reflection

Let's take a moment to reflect on what we just studied.

8. The faithful Creator of the universe cares for you. How does this truth impact you personally?

Application

Now that we better understand the context and meaning of our memory verse, let's apply what we've learned to our own lives.

God teaches us through the apostles Peter and Paul not to take our trials at face value, but instead to view them as spiritual battles.

9. a. How do you currently view and battle your anxieties and fears? Do you take more of a circumstantial or spiritual approach? Or a mix of both?

b. How does knowing that anxiety is first and foremost a spiritual battle change your perspective and battle plan moving forward? What steps will you take today by the power of the Spirit?

10. What anxieties are you currently holding on to? What might it look like to humble yourself before God and surrender your worries and fears to Him?

11. What truths about God will you cling to when you're tempted by anxiety and fear? Where could you write and keep these truths so you can remember them when needed?

Prayer

Take a moment to pray about what you studied. Praise God for who He is, thank Him for what He taught you in this lesson, confess any sins that came to mind, and trust you are forgiven in Christ. Then ask Him to help you apply what you learned to your life in thought and action. Feel free to write that prayer below.

casting all your anxieties on him, because he cares for you

—1 Peter 5:7

Lesson 8

| Memory Verse |

"do not be anxious about anything, but in everything by prayer and supplication with thanksgiving let your requests be made known to God. And the peace of God, which surpasses all understanding, will guard your hearts and your minds in Christ Jesus." — Philippians 4:6–7

Historical Context

Philippians is a letter written by the Apostle Paul to the Philippian church. The city of Philippi was located in Macedonia (present northeastern Greece) and it was there that Paul first established a church in modern-day Europe (Acts 16:6–40). Paul wrote this letter while imprisoned in Rome around 61–62 AD to thank the Philippian believers for their continued support and encourage them in living out their faith.

1. Read Acts 16:25–40. What stands out to you about what Paul and Silas did while imprisoned in Philippi? What was their focus?

Biblical Context

Philippians is a short, four-chapter epistle found in the New Testament after Paul's letter to the Ephesians and before his letter to the Colossians. Philippians is primarily a letter of thanks and encouragement. At the beginning of the epistle, Paul opens with a greeting and prayer. Then he shares about his imprisonment, which leads him to encourage the believers to live out their faith and mature in Christ. In the second half of his letter, he addresses the true gospel and source of righteousness. Then, he closes with more encouragement and thanksgiving—which is the section we will be focusing on.

Read Philippians 4:4–13.

2. Paul emphasizes the importance of rejoicing in verse 4. What do the following verses reveal about our reason for rejoicing and how we can maintain a joyful attitude?

3. List the things Paul instructs believers to think about. What does he say will happen if we think accordingly?

4. In verses 10–12, what did Paul say he learned to do? What is "the secret" or key to learning this?

5. What does this teach you about contentment and how does that encourage you in your struggles with anxiety and fear?

Circumstantial Happiness vs. Spiritual Contentment

Spend time with loved ones, experience new things, find work and hobbies you enjoy, follow your dreams, smile and laugh more. The world offers a lot of advice on how to live a joyful life. These things can make us happier, but they can't guarantee us lasting contentment. Loved ones move or pass away, we aren't always able to do the things we enjoy, and life goals get derailed. Sometimes we go through seasons where there is little circumstantially that makes us smile or laugh.

Paul, on the other hand, was unjustly imprisoned for preaching the gospel and had nearly all of his freedoms stripped from him. And yet, he learned to be content in every circumstance—even in times of hunger and physical need. What was the secret? Jesus. Something that has been consistent as we've read about Paul is that even through intense hardship and imprisonment, his focus remained the same. His eyes were always fixed on Christ and he had wholehearted hope in the gospel.

When we continually preach the gospel to ourselves and seek Jesus through His Word and prayer, we are strengthened by Christ and our joy increases! Believers are not dependent upon circumstances for contentment. Whatever is happening in our lives, we can always rejoice in the gospel and the countless blessings we experience because of what Christ has accomplished for us. Our joy and contentment is found in the certainty that nothing can separate us from the love of God in Christ Jesus our Lord (Romans 8:38–39).

Memory Verse

Let's take a moment to dive a little deeper into our memory verse.

6. How does Paul direct believers to respond to anxiety? How does this relate to Jesus's teaching in Matthew 6:25–34?

7. What does God promise will happen if we follow these commands?

Jesus is Our Peace

Instead of being anxious, we are to pray humbly and earnestly about what we need and give thanks to God for what we have. When we do this, our hearts and minds will be guarded by God's transcending peace in Christ (vv. 6–7). Likewise, we are to continually think godly thoughts and follow the teachings of the Bible. As a result, the God of peace Himself will be with us (vv. 8–9).

But isn't God always with believers? To put it simply, yes. If you believe in Christ's death and resurrection and have turned from your old ways of living to follow Him alone, you have the Holy Spirit dwelling in you (Ephesians 1:13–14). You are positionally at peace with God—declared righteous through Christ—and are forgiven of all of your sins (Romans 5:11). We experience the fullness of His peace when we live in light of this reality.

Jesus said, "Peace I leave with you; my peace I give to you. Not as the world gives do I give to you. Let not your hearts be troubled, neither let them be afraid" (John 14:27). In other words, His all-surpassing peace should impact our anxieties and fears. God is teaching us to pray, give thanks, think about what's true, and live according to His teachings. When we do those things, we will experience a peace unlike anything the world can offer. Peace is always available to those who are at peace with the God of peace.

Reflection

Let's take a moment to reflect on what we just studied.

8. How have your beliefs about joy, contentment, and peace changed after studying this passage?

9. What ways do you need Jesus to guard your heart and mind?

Application

Now that we better understand the context and meaning of our memory verse, let's apply what we've learned to our own lives.

10. What reasons do you have to rejoice that are independent from your circumstances?

11. How will you prioritize praise, prayer, and gratitude in your day-to-day life?

12. a. Are you in control of your thoughts? How would you describe your thought life?

b. Philippians 4:8–9 closely relates to 2 Corinthians 10:5. How is God equipping you to replace anxious thoughts with godly thoughts? What steps will you take to gain control? (See also Galatians 5:22–23, 2 Timothy 1:7, 1 Peter 1:13).

13. Do you trust that Christ can strengthen and teach you to be content in all circumstances? Is there a step you need to take by faith?

Prayer

Take a moment to pray about what you studied. Praise God for who He is, thank Him for what He taught you in this lesson, confess any sins that came to mind, and trust you are forgiven in Christ. Then ask Him to help you apply what you learned to your life in thought and action. Feel free to write that prayer below.

And the peace
of God, which
surpasses all
understanding,
will guard your
hearts and
your minds in
Christ Jesus.
Philippians 4:7

Memory Verse

"The steadfast love of the Lord never ceases; his mercies never come to an end; they are new every morning; great is your faithfulness. 'The LORD is my portion,' says my soul, 'therefore I will hope in him.'"
— *Lamentations 3:22–24*

Historical Context

The Book of Lamentations was written during or shortly after Jerusalem's fall in 586 BC. We don't know for sure who wrote Lamentations, but according to tradition, it was written by the prophet Jeremiah. This is a pretty safe assumption, considering he witnessed Jerusalem's complete destruction and fall to the Babylonians. We also know that God specifically called Jeremiah to have Judah lament (Jeremiah 7:29) and he also wrote laments for King Josiah (2 Chronicles 35:25).[26] The purpose of this book was to express sorrow and grief over what happened in Judah and Jerusalem. Most likely, these poems were meant to be sung or prayed during worship.[27] Still today, Lamentations teaches believers how to biblically process suffering.

1. Read 2 Kings 24:10–17 and 2 Kings 25:8–12. In your own words, describe what happened in Jerusalem. How did this impact the people of Israel?

2. Read 2 Samuel 7:16. What did God promise King David and Israel? How might the fall and exile have confused the Jews who remembered God's covenant? On the other hand, what hope would the promise have given them?

Biblical Context

Lamentations is found in the Old Testament between the books of Jeremiah and Ezekiel. The book contains five poems lamenting Jerusalem's fall and the Babylonian exile. Each poem expresses sorrow and grief over different aspects of this horrific event in Israel's history. We will be focusing on the third poem (chapter 3), where Jeremiah personifies Israel's suffering as a "man who has seen affliction" (Lamentations 3:1). Through this poetic technique, Jeremiah is able to succinctly express the nation's distress, hope, and prayers.

It's important to note that God was judging Israel for generations of idolatry. Their suffering was a direct result of their rebellion against Him. However, not all suffering is a result of God's judgment. In some cases, we suffer the consequences of our own sin like the Jews, but other times we suffer as a result of the sin of others or for completely unknown reasons. Regardless of the cause of your own suffering, we all can learn how to respond and process these complex experiences and emotions biblically by studying Lamentations.

3. a. Read Lamentations 3. Describe the different ways the man expresses his grief.

b. What do you find significant about how he processes what he is feeling and experiencing?

4. a. In your own words, list the ways the man describes his mental and emotional state in verses 17–18.

b. What changes in verse 21? What does the man do and what is the result?

Memory Verse

Let's take a moment to dive a little deeper into our memory verse.

5. What attributes of God's character are described in this passage?

6. What do you think the statement "the LORD is my portion" means for God's people according to these verses? Read Psalm 16:11, Psalm 23, Psalm 73:26, 2 Corinthians 3:5, Ephesians 1:13–14, Philippians 4:19 and 1 Peter 1:3–4.

Our Portion and Inheritance

The Hebrew word for "portion" is *ḥēleq* (khay'lek) and it refers to a share or part in territory.[28] This word is directly linked to the word "inheritance." During Old Testament times, the Israelites would have understood this concept since God had left portions of land to each tribe in the Promised Land and individual families would pass down a land inheritance from generation to generation. However, the Levites were the only tribe that didn't receive an allotment of land. God promised that He would be their portion and inheritance and would provide for their every need (Deuteronomy 10:9).[29] This led the Israelites to the greater truth—that God Himself was their portion and inheritance (Jeremiah 10:16).

Today, this truth applies to all who receive Jesus as Lord and Savior. When we repent and believe in the gospel, we receive the Holy Spirit who lives in us (Galatians 4:6), we're adopted as children of God, and we're considered co-heirs with Christ (Ephesians 3:6). Meaning, God is our portion and inheritance through Christ, who has given us eternal life and grace for today and forever.

7. How does the value of our portion in Christ compare to what the world offers?

8. What impact does recalling all of these truths have on the man?

Satisfy Yourself in Christ

Trusting in Christ as our portion is key to overcoming ongoing battles with anxiety and fear. God wants us to turn to Him when we're struggling. We can bring our brokenness, our cares, and concerns to Him. And while doing so, He wants us to remember who He is and what He promises. Christ's death and resurrection were the ultimate proof that God's love and mercies never end. He is faithful to His character, to His promises, and to His children even unto death. When we put our trust in Jesus, He secures for us an eternal inheritance. This promise gives us hope for the future and also provides hope for today.

Like "the man who has seen affliction," we must choose to hope in our inheritance and be satisfied in Christ as our portion even when we feel unhappy, broken, anxious, and fearful. Notice how in the midst of his emotional turmoil the man calls to mind that which brings him hope and he speaks that truth over himself (Lamentations 3:21, 24). When we're anxious and afraid, we find that recalling who God is, trusting in Him, and rehearsing the truths from God's Word changes everything. Our hope is restored when we satisfy ourselves in Christ and renew our confidence in His faithfulness.

Reflection

Let's take a moment to reflect on what we just studied.

9. God remains faithful to His character and promises. List biblical examples or instances in your own life that remind you of His faithfulness.

Application

Now that we better understand the context and meaning of our memory verse, let's apply what we've learned to our own lives.

10. What does it look like to process suffering biblically? How will this impact how you process anxiety and fear?

11. Are you living as if Christ is truly enough for you? In what ways could a dissatisfaction in Christ be contributing to your anxieties and fears?

12. How will you choose to hope in Christ today even if you are emotionally spent?

Prayer

Take a moment to pray about what you studied. Praise God for who He is, thank Him for what He taught you in this lesson, confess any sins that came to mind, and trust you are forgiven in Christ. Then ask Him to help you apply what you learned to your life in thought and action. Feel free to write that prayer below.

"The LORD is my portion," says my soul therefore I will hope in him.

Lamentations 3:24

Lesson 10

Memory Verse

Is there a memory verse that feels a bit more rusty than the rest? Take a moment to review it.
Feel free to write it out in the space below if that's helpful.

Historical Context

1. Has studying the historical context been a part of your Bible studies in the past? What was your experience with that in this study?

Biblical Context

2. How did studying the biblical context and related verses help you understand the meaning of each memory passage and apply it to your life as you battle anxiety and fear?

Memory Verse

3. How did memorizing verses with each lesson impact you as opposed to simply studying them?

4. Which memory passage had the greatest impact on your anxieties and fears? What was significant about that passage for you?

Reflection

5. Were there any significant moments you want to remember from this study? A specific truth you want to remember? A prayer answered? Something you put into action that led to change? Reflect on those moments below.

6. How have you been impacted by God's grace as you studied, reflected, and began applying what you learned?

7. Which attribute of God gives you the most hope in your battles against anxiety and fear? Why?

8. How has your understanding of anxiety and fear changed over the course of this study?

Application

9. How will you continue to incorporate Scripture memory into your daily life? What are some simple things you can do to learn new verses and review passages you've already memorized?

10. What truths from this study will you rest in when you're feeling anxious and fearful?

11. What will you do today to prepare for future battles against anxiety and fear? Where will you write down key truths and attributes of God so you can easily recall them even if you're struggling mentally?

Prayer

Take a moment to pray about what you studied. Praise God for who He is, thank Him for what He taught you, confess any sins that came to mind, and trust you are forgiven in Christ. Then ask Him to help you apply what you learned to your life in thought and action. Feel free to write that prayer below.

As our confidence in Christ and HIS Word grows, we are STRENGTHENED

Moving Forward

As our confidence in Christ and His Word grows, we are strengthened to face life's ongoing battles against anxiety and fear. I hope you have been increasingly encouraged over the course of this Bible study and that it has spurred you on to continue seeking, trusting, and following Jesus amidst your struggles. It's been a privilege to lead you through these passages and I trust that He is at work in your life because His Word is powerful! I also hope this book you've been writing in has become a keepsake for you to refer to when you need reminders of truth. And of course, as you live out what you learned, remember that you are covered in His perfect grace.

Future Study

If you would like to continue memorizing and studying verses on anxiety and fear, to the right are some more "fighter verses." If you would like to continue in deeper study, the format of this study can be replicated in your personal studies relatively easily. One of the simplest ways you can start studying the historical context, biblical context, and dive deeper into the text is by investing in a good study Bible that provides that information. There are also other great books, commentaries, and free resources available online. If you're not sure where to start, feel free to check out the references I used in this book. And of course, I invite you to follow me at laurenibach.com and subscribe to my mailing list. I love helping women grow closer to Christ and providing weekly encouragement.

Additional Fighter Verses

Old Testament	New Testament
Joshua 1:9	Matthew 6:34
2 Samuel 22:7	John 14:27
Psalm 4:8	John 16:33
Psalm 23:4	Romans 8:28
Psalm 56:3-4	Galatians 2:20
Psalm 94:19	Ephesians 6:12–13
Psalm 139:23–24	2 Corinthians 10:3–5
Proverbs 12:25	Philippians 4:8–9
Isaiah 26:3	Philippians 4:11–13
Isaiah 41:10	2 Timothy 2:1
Isaiah 55:8	1 Peter 5:10
Jeremiah 17:7–8	Revelation 21:4

Lesson 1 Notes

Lesson 2 Notes

Lesson 3 Notes

Lesson 4 Notes

Lesson 5 Notes

Lesson 6 Notes

Lesson 7 Notes

Lesson 8 Notes

Lesson 9 Notes

Lesson 10 Notes

Gratitude

I could not have created this study without Christ equipping and strengthening me each step of the way. He answered many of my prayers for wisdom and guidance through people who were willing to offer their time, wisdom, feedback, or even just a listening ear as I processed all that the Lord was teaching me as I studied and wrote. He deserves all the glory and I wanted to offer my thanks to Him for the individuals He used to help me create this study.

I am grateful to God for Reagan and the team at Paper Peony Press. It has been a privilege to work with them on my first Bible study and I am so thankful for all the work they do behind the scenes so that I can focus on studying, writing, and creating.

I am grateful to God for my husband Luke and his prayers, love, encouragement, and patience with me throughout the creation of this book. Words cannot adequately describe how much I appreciate the countless ways Luke continues to love and support me through every new endeavor and this Bible study was no exception.

I am grateful to God for my mother-in-law, Jeanne. She helped with the vast majority of this study, offering her wisdom from years of teaching the Bible. It was a privilege to learn from her and a gift to receive her encouragement.

I am grateful to God for the loved ones who listened as I processed, offered their wisdom and guidance, and did lessons to give me feedback: Mom, Dad, my sister-in-law Emily, my friends Lauren W., Kristin H. and Deb M., and my pastor Troy and his wife Cheri. And even though I can't name everyone, I am so grateful for all who prayed. I know God heard and answered every prayer.

"I thank my God in all my remembrance of you" — Philippians 1:3

About the Author

Lauren Ibach is an artist and writer with a passion for helping women center their lives on Christ and His Word. She creates hand-lettered artwork, resources, and products to proclaim the gospel and inspire others to love and follow Jesus.

Lauren lives in a suburb near Minneapolis, MN, with her husband Luke. She has been involved in local Bible studies for several years and currently serves in women's ministry at her church. In her free time, Lauren loves spending time at home with her husband and their black cat Layla, and tending to her many plants.

Shop and learn more about Lauren at laurenibach.com.

Scan this code for a closing message from Lauren Ibach!

PLUS ADDITIONAL BONUS!

Please mail reagan@paperpeonypress.com if you're having trouble with the code.

NOTES

Lesson 1

1. Gordon Fee and Douglas Stuart, "The Psalms: Israel's Prayers and Ours," in *How to Read the Bible for All Its Worth* (Grand Rapids, MI: Zondervan, 2014), 212.

2. Strong's Definitions, s.v. "H5337," in *Blue Letter Bible*, accessed April 23, 2022, https://www.blueletterbible.org/lexicon/h5337/esv/wlc/0-2/#lexResults.

3. Strong's Definitions, s.v. in *Blue Letter Bible*, accessed April 23, 2022, https://www.blueletterbible.org/lexicon/h4034/kjv/wlc/0-1.

4. Strong's Definitions, s.v. "H3373," in *Blue Letter Bible*, accessed April 23, 2022, https://www.blueletterbible.org/lexicon/h3373/kjv/wlc/0-1.

Lesson 2

5. Megan Sauter, "Where Is Biblical Colossae?" *Biblical Archaeology Society*, May 20, 2021. https://www.biblicalarchaeology.org/daily/biblical-sites-places/biblical-archaeology-sites/where-is-biblical-colossae/.

6. "Introduction to the Letter of Paul to the Colossians," in *ESV Study Bible*, eds. Lane T. Dennis et al. (Wheaton, IL: Crossway, 2011), 2289–-2292.

Lesson 3

7. "Introduction to the Second Letter of Paul to the Corinthians: 2 Corinthians," in *ESV Study Bible*, eds. Lane T. Dennis et al. (Wheaton, IL: Crossway, 2011), 2219.

8. "Overview: 2 Corinthians," YouTube video, 8:37, posted by BibleProject, November 3, 2016, https://www.youtube.com/watch?v=3lfPK2vfC54&t=314s.

9. "Introduction to the Second Letter of Paul to the Corinthians: 2 Corinthians," in ESV Study Bible, eds. Lane T. Dennis et al. (Wheaton, IL: Crossway, 2011), 2220.

10. John MacArthur, "The First Epistle of Paul to the Corinthians," in *The MacArthur Bible Commentary* (Nashville: Thomas Nelson, 2005), 1561.

11. "Introduction to the First Letter of Paul to the Corinthians: 1 Corinthians," in *ESV Study Bible*, eds. Lane T. Dennis et al. (Wheaton, IL: Crossway, 2011), 2187.

12. "Introduction to the Second Letter of Paul to the Corinthians: 2 Corinthians," in *ESV Study Bible*, eds. Lane T. Dennis et al. (Wheaton, IL: Crossway, 2011), 2222.

Lesson 4

13. Milton Vincent, "My Daily Need," in *A Gospel Primer for Christians* (Bemidji, MN: Focus Publishing, 2008), 14.

14. Matthew Henry, "Introduction to 2 Timothy," in *Blue Letter Bible*, accessed May 4, 2022, https://www.blueletterbible.org/Comm/mhc/2Ti/2Ti_000.cfm?a=1128016.

15. Bill Bright, *How You Can Be Filled With the Holy Spirit* (Orlando, FL: Cru Press, 2019), 26.

Lesson 5

16. John MacArthur, "The Book of Proverbs," in *The MacArthur Bible Commentary* (Nashville: Thomas Nelson, 2005), 695.

17. Strong's Definitions, s.v. "H2451," in *Blue Letter Bible*, accessed May 11, 2022, https://www.blueletterbible.org/lexicon/h2451/kjv/wlc/0-1/.

18. "Overview: Proverbs," YouTube video, 8:07, posted by BibleProject, May 31, 2016, https://www.youtube.com/watch?v=AzmYV8GNAIM&t=399s

19. Strong's Definitions, s.v. "H3820," in *Blue Letter Bible*, accessed May 11, 2022, https://www.blueletterbible.org/lexicon/h3820/kjv/wlc/0-1.
20. Strong's Definitions, s.v. "H982," in *Blue Letter Bible*, accessed May 10, 2022, https://www.blueletterbible.org/lexicon/h982/kjv/wlc/0-1.

Lesson 6
21. John MacArthur, "Introduction to the Gospels," in *The MacArthur Bible Commentary* (Nashville: Thomas Nelson, 2005), 1095.
22. John MacArthur, "The Gospel According to Matthew," in *The MacArthur Bible Commentary* (Nashville: Thomas Nelson, 2005), 1128.
23. Strong's Definitions, s.v. "G3640," in *Blue Letter Bible*, accessed May 13, 2022, https://www.blueletterbible.org/lexicon/g3640/niv/mgnt/0-1.

Lesson 7
24. John MacArthur, "The First Epistle of Peter," in *The MacArthur Bible Commentary* (Nashville: Thomas Nelson, 2005), 1921.
25. Strong's Definitions, s.v. "G5013," in *Blue Letter Bible*, accessed May 18, 2022, https://www.blueletterbible.org/lexicon/g5013/kjv/tr/0-1.

Lesson 9
26. John MacArthur, "The Book of Lamentations," in *The MacArthur Bible Commentary* (Nashville: Thomas Nelson, 2005), 883.
27. "Introduction to Lamentations," in *ESV Study Bible*, eds. Lane T. Dennis et al. (Wheaton, IL: Crossway, 2011), 1476.
28. Strong's Definitions, s.v. "H2506," in *Blue Letter Bible*, accessed May 26, 2022, https://www.blueletterbible.org/lexicon/h2506/esv/wlc/0-1.
29. "What does it mean to say that God is my portion?," Got Questions, accessed May 26, 2022, https://www.gotquestions.org/God-is-my-portion.html.